Professional Guide For Setting Up Internet Business/Make Money Online

By
Christopher Obiaku
Internet Business Professional

Notice

Meanwhile, with regards to offering great customer care service, my contacts are attached below so you can easily reach me with any of your questions. I believe as a starter or intermediate, you might have one or two questions and I will be pleased to have it all well addressed so you can progress with your internet business.

In addition, if you had hoped to operate an internet business all these while but doesn't know how, just relax and be happy, why, because the book will lead you every step of the way in establishing good internet business up till when it starts generating huge income.

Phone numbers: +2348036953673, +2348095854528
E-mail: chrisbusinessacademy@yahoo.com
www.ChrisBusinessAcademy.com

Introduction

Unemployment as well as lack of financial freedom is presently a curse all over the world, leading our youths into all forms of bad social vices; males engage in crimes while the females are good with prostitution exposing themselves to high risk of death, diseases and abuse.

The above theory inspired the quest for new sources of making money for, which the internet serves as the best alternative taking into the consideration the millions of people that uses the internet for various transactions since the world is transforming into a global village. The unavailability of jobs as well as the quest for making extra income in form of diversification has raised the level of internet users, who sets up online business in order to make extra income. With internet business there are all possibilities of making good more money online, which serves as serves as the new market for marketing and selling of goods and services at a large volume.

In addition, despite the fact that lots of money can be made online with internet business it can also be a total failure if online business ethics are not maintained and applied, which is exactly where the eBook plays a great role.

"Professional Guide For Setting up Internet Business/Make Money Online" was writing out of experience by decisively addressing the technicalities involved in making money online through the various well analyzed ways of earning money on the internet. This is to help you have a hitch-free process in setting up internet business as well as make money online. These involve what to do and what not to do.

The book is meant to serve as empowerment resources, which will extensively assist in alleviating the high level of unemployment and financial handicap. The eBook will empower people financially through the step by step guide and directions till a successful internet business is established as well as starts making money online.

Chapter One

What is online business?

Meanwhile, internet or online business also referred to as e-business (E- for electronic) can be seen as that aspect of business, which transactions is mostly carried out on the internet. Any form of business activity performed within the internet is online business. So if you carry out any form of money making activity on the internet then, you are operating internet business. This is supplemented with online payment processor systems (Internet Banks), like perfect money, PayPal, webmoney, netteller to name but few, which makes online transactions easy and possible.

The globalization of the world powered by discovery of the internet, initiated the establishment of the booming new market (The Internet) just like it was to Europe during the discovery of the "New Market"

(Americas) many centuries ago since they were in need of market where they can sell their products and services. The ability to communicate with people easily online as well as carry out transactions made it possible for internet business to boom. With the help of the internet business people can purchase goods and services within the comfort of their homes, which is well patronized now since people can hardly deal with the stress of offline/traditional markets especially the working class; time/burden of driving or walking to market, going store by store searching for needed goods and services. So it's for the seller who don't have to make money only offline but online too since offline products and services can easily be marketed as well as sold. All done within the internet and without any physical contact unlike daily purchases where human physical contact is necessary before transaction can be carried out as well as successful.

Discovery of e-business led to the possibility of making money online majorly through marketing of one product or the other as to generate sales and money, which serves as a great alternative to the stress of daily jobs; walking back and forth everyday to work, boss unending nagging and disturbance, lack of self ascertained free time. With online business, you are your own boss and answerable to no one, it's also at your discretion to choose what time to work and can be done at the comfort of your home without any disturbance.

In addition, to making money online, make sure to be prepared as well as better guided since making money online is presently, highly competitive, which implies that only those that understands how it works can succeed with it. Making money online could be stressful sometimes as well as sometime involves capital investment but it's worth the stress when the income starts coming, which is non-stop.

Chapter Two

Step By Step Guide To Setting Up Internet Business

Meanwhile, internet business is the new market for making more money by either promoting individual or partners products or services.

Further, to start a successful and flourishing online business that can be generating lots of income for you, there is need to understand as well as apply the five processes of executing business projects, which are majorly five in number, which comprises:-

1. IDEAS INITIATION

This is the stage where you reflect on the type of business to set up on the internet as to start making money online. This must be based on a niche, domain, product and services you are passionate and well informed about. This is necessary so you can defend as well as write well on it when the need arises since it's possible that you customers might have few questions for you with regards to the business as it affects them. And when you cannot explain to their understanding, it might cost you clients as they might leave and never come back. In addition, to that, in the course of promoting the chosen domain, you needs to write original articles for your website, comment on forums or social media on the choosing niche. These shows that your ability to fully understand your money making channel and business field is a must or you might fail after you must have waste your time and resources.

These might sound a bit difficult to achieve since many goes into online business just to make money and nothing else; not even the chosen domain. To get a good domain/niche or name for your business, first of all, sat down and reflect on something you love to do even if you are not paid for it. That's the secret, why, because, it could generally come to a point where you might be like I can't move on anymore. Is natural for starters but your passion for it even without payment can help you withstand the predicament for that moment and it can serve as an exceptional encouragement. For example; imagine, you love to take pictures and in other to monetize the talent you established a website where you sale photos or make money hope to make money from it through Google adsense and affiliate marketing. Do think that for the moment, the website had not started generating income, will stop you from taking pictures and stockpiling your website. No! That's because your passion is for taking pictures, which serves as your first priority while making money out of it becomes secondary. It can be a priority too but never a passion. If money comes first especially when it's the field you did not master well, the business might fail since the foundation pillars are not strong. Make sure the money making Idea you choose it part of your hobby, which is unlimitedly within and not borrowed idea. When choose the wrong internet business idea, you can easily be discouraged during the hard times if you operate on a niche/domain/product and services you don't have passion for since the drive, is to make money and when it's not forthcoming you drop out, which is natural too because you cannot do what you don't know thereby wasting your time and money for nothing compared to when you might had started with the niche or domain you love as well as cherished. Never base your establishment of internet business on the passion of making money, though, it's important but should not be the priority because when you don't see the money, you get tired and fold up, that's how many fails and looks for whom to blame. Please, never choose to start an internet business on a particular field because your friend is making money with it. There is no guarantee that since it works for your friend so will it work for you. Your friend might be very conversant with the field, which are the things to need to find out before copying. Do promote a business niche you know very well or you fail.

2. PLANNING

This is another vital stage to note while establishing online business. Nevertheless, after you must had researched and find the online business idea you love to operate on, comes planning. Every business; internet business inclusive must have business plans and requirements, which must be achieved for there to be success. You can even write a business proposal on it for better articulation and comprehension. Writing it down will help you discover any missing link compared to when you are imaging it on your mind. The below question can help;

1. How well do you know the selected business idea?

2. What's the competition like and how will you overcome it?
3. What are the likely financial costs for the online business and how can you afford it?
4. What's your believe the business will succeed?
5. How do you cope with the venture in times of difficulty or stress of not going forward?

You can better establish a great internet business opportunity that will be making lots of money for you online if you can be able to answer the above questions decisively before starting an online business investment. Do not rush it but take your time to do a great research since it's a long term program that will be generating extra income for you. The financial benefits of any successful online business are worth the early stage stress of setting it up. Mind you, any mistake that takes place here might affect its success along the line.

3. EXECUTION

The execution stage is very sensitive since this is why time and resources will be fully involved. Prior to embarking on execution of your business idea findings you MUST had certified the success and technicalities of the business following your research findings during planning. This is where you start designing your web page, which could website or blog, write as well as compile original articles on your selected niche with good search keywords. That will help boost the web page search engine ranking on Google, bing est. if the website is already designed and hosted; this is where you start building backlinks by posting articles on social media and public forums with redirection link back to your website as well as promoted product and services. Also make sure to advertize your links on platforms that has everything in common with what you are promoting so you can have the right traffic/visitors or clients whose impact can amount to sales and money.

4. MONITORING AND CONTROL

These must be observed as long as the business lasts since it's clear that no business activity can survive if not monitored and controlled from time to time as to adapt to change, which is constant. This is where you must have set up the business, then use monitoring and control to put it under serious check so it doesn't fade away or fail. These can be done by updating and reviewing the website articles as to be in line with new searched ideas, formulating new policies to guide the business operation and growth as well as to meets reigning standard. It advisable to implement new ideas so as to stand out during competition of that niche on the internet, which is very active now due to numerous businesses been established on the internet.

Many people presently, believes in online business and its financial freedom thereby establishing internet businesses of all sort everyday, which makes competition very tight. Once the monitoring and control stops, the business could die off because one thing is constant and that is change so for the online business venture to survive it must be well monitored and controlled by formulating and implementing new policies and ideas as to match with the environmental changes and ideology.

5. CLOSURE

This is where you start the documenting process by storing the business start up resources like written materials, software est. for future reference purposes. After, which you can take up another type of internet business to establish and before you know it, you would had established lots of internet businesses making thousands of dollars for you on daily, weekly and monthly basis.

Chapter Three

Ways to make money online
With Internet Business

The internet is presently one of
the best recommended ways of
earning lots of money without
much stress compared to
struggling as an employee on
daily basis with nothing to show

for it. Depending on your time, talents and dedication, you can engage in lots of online money making channels but it's good to take it one after another. That will help you understand the business very well before moving to another establishment of internet business.

With regards to means of making money online, there are various ways of achieving it depends on your passion, talent and time.

Stated and analyzed below are the ways of making money online from all around the globe with just a laptop and internet connection.

1. Affiliate Marketing
2. Google ad sense
3. Blogging
4. Designing and hosting Website
5. Freelancing
6. Website

Step by step guide to making money online with affiliate marketing.

What Is Affiliate Marketing
Affiliate marketing simply means creating awareness of business partner's product and services

so as to generate sales for, which some percentage of commission are paid after sales is confirmed. How much you make with affiliate marketing depends on how many sales your links confirmed. Don't be confused, this is done invincibly online but there are tools and software used to monitor activities of the affiliate links. You can also install your own monitoring tools too for accuracy sake since some affiliate companies can be dubious. That will help avoid discrepancies or cheats during payment. Meanwhile, following the boost of internet business, affiliate marketing plays a great role in helping people make lots of extra income through promotion of affiliates (partners) products and services for a commission.

Affiliate marketing is an online business, which afford individuals the opportunity of generating huge income by creating awareness of particular products and services. Here, money in form of commission can only be made when product or services is sold and money confirmed through your link. This is why you need to be very careful with the accuracy of the link you promote because a single missing word can re-direct it to another source. And once it can't be traced to your link then, you've lost it and the commission of the sales. So monitor your advert links very well before publishing.

How Affiliate Marketing Works
1. Affiliate obtains a web page (Website or free blog)
2. Affiliate displays adverts of partner products or services on their web page
3. Customer/visitor clicks on the advert or link
4. Customer is re-directed to the merchant website through tracking link

5. Client buys goods and services from the major company website

6. Company affiliate network records the transaction and details of sales

7. The purchase as well as transaction is confirmed as valid sales

8. The referring affiliate is credited with the transaction and commission is paid out.

The system is very simply and stress-free; no stress of shipping, product or customer care handling. All need to be done is to promote the product or service links issued.

This can be done through the social media, online communities and forums. With the level of increase on internet users every day since the world is turning into a global village, imagine how much you can make by promoting those products or services owing to the huge number of internet users, which cuts across the globe.

Chapter Four

Step By Step Guide To Setting Up Affiliate Marketing

Before we start, first find out, which platform or web page you might want to use; free blog or paid web page. If free blog, you can use wordpress or Google

BlogSpot. You can either chose blogspot or wordpress or both depending on your time in making them active always. The registration will take but few minutes and make sure you register with your chosen domain name just that it won't end with .com anymore but .wordpress.com (example; free blog domain name goes like this (wwwDOTmakemoneyDOTwordpressDOTcom) compared to wwwDOTmoneyonlineDOTcom for paid website. Many prefer the second because of its originality, which boost customer's confidence and clicks attraction. In addition, the easy flow of the name and unallowed displayed of ads compared to free blogs makes it outstanding.

Guide For Using Paid Option
In case you want to change your free domain name to paid domain name, just click or copy and paste the link on your browser but if it's on print copy, please, do type the link words as it appears on your browser as to register with **dream host;** a world rated, awesome web hosting company. The link will give you the opportunity of registering your own domain name at about 90 percent discount for one year, which I

believe is enough for starter to test the market. The normal monthly fee is $8 per month, which amounts to $96 per year but with my link, you will have it at $1.99 per month and $23.88 for just one year. I had to pay the hidden charges so you can have a test of how fruitful the internet business because I believe that before the expiration of the one year, you must had generated lots of income to pay up the other year. But if you don't need the bonus and wants to host at normal monthly rate, do use the link here. In addition, also know that I had to reduce the price so you don't make mistake of falling into the hands of low quality cheap hosting company as a starter with low budget. I don't think you will like your website to spent minutes before it boost when someone clicks on it. Definitely, the visitor will stop and switch to the next website on the search list neither will you be happy to have an urgent issue that needs to be resolved within 5 hours and yet after 24 hours the issue is not fixed. Definitely the website will go down. Also I don't think you will like to wake up to see that your website content is all gone and crashed. Those are the more

reasons why an internet establisher must highly consider the hosting company, which manages the presence of the website on the internet making it a big player in part of website success.
Do endeavor to host with my link as a thank you for the idea.

Back To Using Free Blog

When you are through registering with blogger.com or wordpress.com and obtained your login details, login to design your web page to your test. Newbie might think it difficult but don't bother for you must not be an expert to know it. Go to the admin and use the settings, appearance, widgets, themes and so many others to design your blog outlooks. Though, it's not a must but necessary so it will look more attractive and adoring to visitors who might want to come back again.

When you are done with the design, the next thing is to start publishing articles with good pictures on the blog based on your chosen domain, niche. Please make sure you post original articles with good search keywords. Do not copy other peoples work because Google and other search engines can find out and suspend your account making all your effort so far a waste. In addition to that, publishing copyrighted articles on your blog will also destroy its position on search engines and make it hard to be found when people search for ideas or topics relating to your articles or website. And before you know it, it dies off as you will be tired of wasting your time waiting to see the money come. Imagine that the internet had first captured and ranked the first published article, what do you think will become of your website or blog when search engine monitoring tools dictates such duplicate on your web page having been programmed to punish defaulters. Those search engines are programmed software and when they are instructed to dictate and devalue website with copyrighted works, exactly that will they do. So be careful about posting copyrighted works thinking that no one will know, even if you cannot write, you can hire someone else. It's just that you need to spend some little money though; the financial freedom from the website is worth it when income starts flowing in. If you do not have time to write or not good

at writing, like I said earlier, feel free to contact me, mind you, you need to have a copyright website or software for testing the originality of the articles before making payment since some freelancers now use cheat software to write.
www.copyscape.com is the best for testing articles originality and make sure it's not a copyrighted work. In addition to that, please, publish articles as many as possible on your selected niche, domain, product and services.

When you are done with publishing articles with beautiful and quality pictures by then, the website and its domain name might had lasted for few weeks or months preferably, on the internet. Next, is to start making money with affiliate marketing by registering with affiliate marketing companies. Your web page will serve as your store front, which will make them not to delay in accepting you into their affiliate system. Abuse of the system is making companies to be elective of their affiliate marketers so as to protect their mage. This is why I advice that your blog should look attractive and qualitative so the wont doubt accepting you since the web page is what really matters to them. That's why some affiliate companies makes it a must priority for acceptance into their affiliate marketing system.

Furthermore, when you must have applied and accepted as affiliate, login into your affiliate account and click at the promotion tab. That's where all ads resources like banners, campaigns and product and services links are published. When there, search for the links, banners and campaigns of product or services you hope to promote. Make sure to select product or services ads that are attractive and clear or people might not click at it. Copy the advert link and post on your website or blog mostly positioned at the right or left side bar for easy view and click though; you can choose to publish it anywhere you like within your website or blog space. In addition to posting it on your website or blog, you can also publish it in your articles too. Within your article perhaps, at the top or center of each topic of your published articles but make sure the advertized link showcase partially if not fully what the visitor or reader hopes

to take a look at if not no one
will click on your adverts.

What to do lastly to start making
money when you must had
published few ads on your
website or blog is promotion.
Mind you, don't be greedy of
making too much money at the
start up thereby compiling your
website or blog with all kinds of
affiliate links. Some uses cheats
but it will to a large extend
devalue your website on search
engines if not suspended. Start
with few affiliate ads and expand
when you start gaining internet
exposure and traffic. Even one
Ad that's well promoted can earn

you six figure incomes in future, is all about your time and dedication.

Next after you must have installed all your ads is to promote it and see how money is made online. You will be surprise to see how money from sales commission will be compiling in your account even as you sleep. That's if you promote it decisively the right way rather than utilizing illegal cheats and robots. The impact you make in promoting your web page determines how much you make. So endeavor to create large awareness about your blog, website and product and services you market. Just have your link anywhere you are.

Chapter Five

Ways To Promote Affiliate Marketing Links

Analyzed below are the various means of creating large awareness creation of your website. In addition to those analyzed on this chapter, there is a comprehensive list at the last chapter for promoting your website.

1.   Keyword Articles

To drastically increase your website or blog exposure and search engine rank on the internet, make sure to keep publishing original articles on it. You need to write or employ someone else to write original articles for you perhaps, reviewing your website and the product and services it promotes using good search keywords. For better understanding of the activeness of keywords in search engines; for example if words that are well search online by people depending on your niche is "How to lose weight" which records 80 percent clicks while "Ways to lose weight" records 50 percent. Definitely, it's obvious that if your writer does not understands that and keeps using ways to lose weight so will it be having 50 percent view compared to when joined with "How to lose weight. That's just an example for it can come in many forms; it could used in form of single word. For example; "A" have more click percentage compared to "An" which is why you see many writers use "A" rather "AN" before a vowel sound (e.g. "An" aeroplane is now changed to "A" aeroplane). Though, it's an English error but the writer needs the clicks and search engine rank upgrade. Those are the technicalities of promoting website or blog I want you to understand because those are the success of all the successful website you saw online making thousands of dollars. You can better imagine how much clicks or internet traffic and money your website or blog could be generating on daily, weekly or monthly basis if it's published with articles that reflects the above idea. That will not only boost your sales income, it will also rank your website position high on search engines like Google, bing e.t.c. And when it happens, you won't have to source for customers or clients anymore as they will keep coming through the established tactics and so is the payment too.

2. Join Online Forums/Communities

Participating actively on internet forums and discussion communities is one of the ways of directing customers and traffic to your online business blog. Though, you MUST make sure to join public communities or forums that deal on what you promote so you can be interacting with likeminded individuals. Don't promote weight loss products or services and go join political forum to discuss weight loss issues. That might not work or generate the needed customer because you will like who visits your blog or website today to come back again, which is why you need to know what they want and post exactly that they wish to read or see.

This is how you can generate customers and traffic by joining forums pertaining to your niche. Public forums are were people interacts as well as seek information so let's say you promote as well as maintain a blog on weight loss and having registered with a particular forum it must happen that within all the posted threads, some might have issues or questions about how to lose weight or burn fat. Being that the topic is what you are well conversant with as well as covers what your web page promotes, what you do is to explain in brief about the asked question on the forum, then, leave behind a re-direct link to an article on your website where the question is fully explained. Once you had the right answers, the person asking the question and people that might hope to have such question answered must definitely keep clicking on the link you left behind so as to read and understand more. Imagine how much customer and money you can be making on daily, weekly and monthly basis consistently if you are able to share as well as post your links to lots of public forums.

In addition to answering people's questions, you can write a review with links about the product and services your website or blog promotes and publish it on forum too so people can easily click as the read.

Further, so how do you get the websites of forums where to share your links and posts? What to do is go to google.com search engine and search for forum websites based on your domain. For example if your website is about weight loss search for weight loss forums, which you can easily generate by typing "Best weight loss forums" on Google and click search. Google will display lots of forums on weight loss, you can checkmate the ones with good traffic and write them down and register later or you can click and register right away but endeavor to visit the forum once in a while as to comments and spread your links until it starts attracting visitors or traffic on its own. This is why you must understand your selected niche very well so you can freely write on it always.

3. Write your website or blog link anywhere possible

Physically, you can create mini sign board, banners and leaflets with you domain name clearly written on it, advertizing the product and services your web page promotes. These can be pasted on the walls of people crowded places. It can be shared to people as well as left behind perhaps, in a bus as you come out e.t.c. make sure the internet link is clearly displayed on it. Even if you cannot afford money for the advert expenses. Chalk or charcoal should be enough to help you write the link on walls of crowded place like markets, parks, roads. It can be better down at night or earliest morning to avoid public notice. Know that with the level at, which people have access to internet so will the easily copy the link and checked it out for, which there are possibility the clicks can turn to sales and money.

4. Social Media

I believe you have account with the social media like face book, LinkedIn, twitter, which now plays a great role in generating huge traffics to websites/blog. Just the way you update your status on social media, channel your writings towards your website article link, you can also share all your articles on your social media for which only the topics will be displayed and who wants to read more must click on it to be directed to your website. It's advisable you create a new page for the website or blog using its domain name then add as much people as you can as well as encourage them to share your post so it can be seen by their own networks, who can connect with your activity. Spreading your link must be your priority since there lays the future benefits and success of any internet website and business. Write, write and write

Chapter Six

How To Make Money Online With Google Adsense

What is Google adsense?

Google adsense is a program established by Google, which sees to the financial rewards as well as payment of clients promoting Google paid ads either on their websites or blog. With Google adsense unlike affiliate marketing, there is no need to make sales before money can be made. You start earning incomes into your account once someone clicks on Google ads displayed on your website or blog. It happens that due to Google's large search engine network, People pay them for advert of their website links or goods and services. Google on its part is willing to share the percentage of the money with you if only people can click the ads through your web page thereby expanding the advertized goods and services as well as links. it might seems so simply and also a waste of money from the advertiser when compared to affiliate marketing where sales must be recorded before commission can be paid. That shows that advertising comes in many forms and the advertizing agreement between Google and the client is that money should be paid once the advert links are clicked. So whether the visitor makes any purchases or not having clicked on the ads is none of the hired advertiser or Google's business. That is why Google seriously punishes defaulters as well as do not tolerate cheats like people clicking or paying individuals to click on ads displayed on their web page. This is because it's not fair to the client that paid for the advert. One bad thing about it, is that the system cannot dictate the legal and illegal clicks, so you can click on your ads and gets paid but Google will find out when the wants to pay you. The money will be seized and sent back to the client. For example; like you clicking the ads, definitely it's obvious, you have no intention of buying anything but gets paid when clicked on the ads. That makes fool of Google and the paid advertiser, which is why Google don't waste time in suspending accounts found in such activities. The advertisement is meant to be clicked by individuals who really need the information as well as possible buyers, which is why it's posted on websites based on what the website promotes so as to have the right traffic. In addition, do know that no commission or payment is accredited to sales recorded with the advert. So should the visitor clicks on the link and later make purchases of lots of goods or services, all the earnings are for

the benefit of the main
advertiser.

The internet business economy
is worth trillions of dollars due to
the level of its users around the
globe and Google adsense is one
of the ways of making money
from the business online. The
difference between affiliate
marketing and Google adsense
is that, unlike affiliate marketing
there is no need to record sales
before getting paid. You get paid
once the links are clicked but the
bad part is that should the
visitor make purchases of goods
and services worth thousands of

dollars, you will have no single commission for the sales. With Google adsense there is no limit to how much thousands of dollars one can make on daily, weekly or monthly bases. With Google adsense there is no product to market or sale before making money. You get paid once visitor's clicks on the Google adverts installed on your web page.

Newbie or some people might wonder how possible it's with regards to how the advertiser and Google make money to foot those bills but they are at the enjoying end. The client believes that from the clicks sales can be generated. And the Google advert for Pay per View (PPV) fee is far lower compared to the how much that will be paid out based on commission. That's paying onetime fee for general sales compared to paying commission on any single sales. That's the secret and it's a too way thing since it's possible there will be clicks but there won't be sales and that's lost, it can also happen the other way round.

Google on its part as a marketing and advertizing firm, which hopes to reach its customers goal of wide range exposure and awareness creation of clients products and services on the internet, decides to share a percentage of the paid services fee with you. That's if you can only promote the clients links to products and services on your website. For example, the advert client pays Google 10 dollar to promote the ads using their search engine platform, it could be Pay per Click (PPC) and Pay per View (PPV) depending on the advertiser's choice during registration. The ten dollars can generate thousands of dollars in return or otherwise. Google on its quest expose to widely advertize the links, goods or services by far and wide, pays you like 4 dollars out of the 10 dollars for each ads clicked through your website or blog. Like I said earlier, the clients advertizing as well as agreement with Google was not that goods must be sold before money can be earned. Clients pays for people to view their product and services links and should the visitor make purchases later becomes the benefit of the main advertiser but you must have being paid for the first click through your website or blog. This is why Google deals severely with people that click at their own link.

The paid advertiser pays to have the right customer clicks on the links which might turn to sales. So when you click at your own link and gets paid it's a cheat because it's a waste of money. So never click on your own ads because Google will suspend your account right away and that's a sign of good reputation from Google in protecting their customer's interest and that of their company.

There is no need to cheat on it because you will regret it if caught. I speak out of a experience; it will seems sweet when you see the money compiling on your account as you click but Google will freeze it out during payment since the traffic direction was from one direction. Think of how much you could be making when you promote your website or blog and have the right visitors clicking on it on your web pages. Mind you again, Google have great software monitoring all these promotion and financial activities as to checkmate abuse and crime.

Chapter Seven

STEP BY STEP GUIDE TO SETTING IT UP

Further, to make money with online with Google ad sense, you must have a landing page like website or blog, which Google will use to identify you as well as where they can display the ads. Is not like affiliate marketing where you are issued links. And you can copy share on forums and social media and make money but on Google adsense you must have your own landing page; website or blog where Google can install the ads as well as track the links clicked through your website or blog. This is why Google created BlogSpot for establishment of free blog whose domain name must end with blogspotDotCom for example, if your chosen blog name is wwwDotweightlossDotcom with free Google blogger the name will be wwwDotweightlossDotblogspotDotcom.

Google invented the program as to help many that cannot afford money for websites, which brings in the idea of making money online for free, why, because everything is totally free. The landing page should had required money to design since website costs but with the free blog promotion is nothing and can be done individually unless you want to outsource it but it's totally free to set up and operate.

Nevertheless, when you must had created your free blog, like I said earlier you can design a good free blog with Google BlogSpot www.blogger.com or www.wordpress.com and when it's ready with few articles and photos on it, proceed to register with Google adsense program. When you apply Google will go through your profile especially your blog, so make it ok. Once its certified and accepted into Google adsense program, Google will start publishing ads on it which, can be on the left, right or center side bar of the blog depending on where you set it to be posted. Make sure it's where people can easily see and click it. That's it, so whenever someone clicked on the Google ads marketed on your web page, you get paid. The visitor doesn't have to make purchases of goods and services through the link before money can be made. You get paid once the link is clicked on.

Lastly, it's important to note that how much you make with your blog depends on how much traffic you generate, so in order to make much money online you need to promote the blog and it can be promoted exactly as that of affiliate marketing links, which is below

1. Social Media

I believe you have account with the social media like face book, LinkedIn, twitter, which now plays a great role in generating huge traffics to websites/blog. Just the way you update your status on social media, channel your writings towards your website article link, you can also share all your articles on your social media for which only the

topics will be displayed and who wants to read more must click on it to be directed to your website. It's advisable you create a new page for the website or blog using its domain name then add as much people as you can as well as encourage them to share your post so it can be seen by their own networks, who can connect with your activity. Spreading your link must be your priority since there lays the future benefits and success of any internet website and business.
Write, write and write.

2.   Keyword Articles

To drastically increase your website or blog exposure and search engine rank on the internet, make sure to keep publishing original articles on it. You need to write or employ someone else to write original articles for you perhaps, reviewing your website and the product and services it promotes using good search keywords. For better understanding of the activeness of keywords in search engines; for example if words that are well search online by people depending on your niche is "How to lose weight" which records 80 percent clicks while "Ways to lose weight" records 50 percent. Definitely, it's obvious that if your writer does not understands that and keeps using ways to lose weight so will it be having 50 percent view compared to when joined with "How to lose weight. That's just an example for it can come in many forms; it could used in form of single word. For example; "A" have more click percentage compared to "An" which is why you see many writers use "A" rather "AN" before a vowel sound (e.g. "An" aeroplane is now changed to "A" aeroplane). Though, it's an English error but the writer needs the clicks and search engine rank upgrade. Those are the technicalities of promoting website or blog I want you to understand because those are the success of all the successful website you saw online making thousands of dollars. You can better imagine how much clicks or internet traffic and money your website or blog could be generating on daily, weekly or monthly basis if it's published with articles that reflects the above idea. That will not only boost your sales income, it will also rank your website position high on search engines like Google, Bing e.t.c. And when it happens, you won't have to source for customers or clients anymore as they will keep coming through the established tactics and so is the payment too.

3. Join Online Forums/Communities

Participating actively on internet forums and discussion communities is one of the ways of directing customers and traffic to your online business blog. Though, you MUST make sure to join public communities or forums that deal on what you promote so you can be interacting with likeminded individuals. Don't promote weight loss products or services and go join political forum to discuss weight loss issues. That might not work or generate the needed customer because you will like who visits your blog or website today to come back again, which is why you need to know what they want and post exactly that they wish to read or see.

This is how you can generate customers and traffic by joining forums pertaining to your niche.

Public forums are were people interacts as well as seek information so let's say you promote as well as maintain a blog on weight loss and having registered with a particular forum it must happen that within all the posted threads, some might have issues or questions about how to lose weight or burn fat. Being that the topic is what you are well conversant with as well as covers what your web page promotes, what you do is to explain in brief about the asked question on the forum, then, leave behind a re-direct link to an article on your website where the question is fully explained. Once you had the right answers, the person asking the question and people that might hope to have such question answered must definitely keep clicking on the link you left behind so as to read and understand more. Imagine how much customer and money you can be making on daily, weekly and monthly basis consistently if you are able to share as well as post your links to lots of public forums.

In addition to answering people's questions, you can write a review with links about the product and services your website or blog promotes and publish it on forum too so people can easily click as the read.

Further, so how do you get the websites of forums where to share your links and posts? What to do is go to google.com search engine and search for forum websites based on your domain. For example if your website is about weight loss search for weight loss forums, which you can easily generate by typing "Best weight loss forums" on Google and click search. Google will display lots of forums on weight loss, you can checkmate the ones with good traffic and write them down and register later or you can click and register right away but endeavor to visit the forum once in a while as to comments and spread your links until it starts attracting visitors or traffic on its own. This is why you must understand your selected niche very well so you can freely write on it always.

4. Write your website or blog link anywhere possible

Physically, you can create mini sign board, banners and leaflets with you domain name clearly written on it, advertizing the product and services your web page promotes. These can be pasted on the walls of people crowded places. It can be shared to people as well as left behind perhaps, in a bus as you come out e.t.c. make sure the internet link is clearly displayed on it. Even if you cannot afford money for the advert expenses, Chalk or charcoal should be enough to help you write the link on walls of crowded place like markets, parks, roads. It can be better down at night or earliest morning to avoid public notice. Know that with the level at, which people have access to internet so will the easily copy the link and checked it out for, which there are possibility the clicks can turn to sales and money.

Chapter Eight

How To Make Money Online With Website/blog

Meanwhile, if you don't have a website/blog or have a website and you are not making money on the internet with it then, you are really missing it. You need money for your website hosting and maintenance fees unless, you are using a free blog, which still needs maintenance.

A website or free blog is a good platform of generating extra income through the internet owing to the positive impact the posses on internet business, which serves as an e-store business.
Making money online with Google adsense works best with a landing page like website or blog. Once someone clicks on the Google adverts displayed on your website, you get paid. Here, there is no need to sell any product as to earn commission. You make money

when the advertized link is clicked.

Secondly, is affiliate marketing, a website or blog is a good ways of promoting or creating awareness of a product or services. All you need do is research a good reputable affiliate marketing company, register with them and use your website or blog as sales front, choose the products or services of affiliate market network group that has everything in common with your website, copy their links and promote them either through your website articles, web page front. That's all. Keep generating visitors and so will the finance keep flowing in. Thirdly is an advertisement fee from public or private companies/individuals. You will notice that once your website or blog is well noticed on the internet and its search rank on search engines has increased people will start contacting you. This is for you to advertize their product or services on your web page for a paid fees, which you can decide depending on the level of your website advancement online.

You can better imagine how much you can be making with your website or blog when the several installed links are welcoming lots of visitors/traffics and clients. Own a web page today.

Make Money Writing EBook Or Software's

EBook means electronic book; that is, books that can be sold in soft copy and can only be read on computers, tablets or mobile phone. Unlike hard copies that can be felt and sold physically, EBooks can only be downloaded online, which saves stress of handling hard copies, which includes production and shipping.

Presently, it's obvious that people all over the world faces one challenges or the other and are in serious need of one information or the other as a solution to their problems. These people are also ready to pay for the information so far as it meets their needs as well as worth it.

With that been said, following the various information people needs why not seat down and think of anyone to write and sell it to make money. People seeks information on how to make money online, some needs information on weight loss and so on. First identify the topic and information you are good at then write it as an eBook and start selling. Mind you, you must be a good writer as to be able to write a good and patronized eBook. For those that cannot write, there is hope as you can compile needed information's as an eBook and start selling but never duplicate copyrighted works as it will bounce back on you if the original owner finds out. There are free non copyrighted works you can use to make up your eBook.

Below is the step by step guide to getting started

First, like I said earlier, think of information you can write very well e.g. entrepreneurship, weight loss e.t.c. Even if you cannot write endeavor to have the idea so you can be able to compile awesome need information by your customers because when the buy your product and testifies it goodness then, your business finance will boost for people like what is tried and test. And I don't think you will love to make only first sale and no more. That's how insincere internet business owners see it. No minding that using fake activities can stop someone from not coming back. Nobody that experiences any form of scam or irregularity on a website will like to go back there, not after the huge competition. The person won't come back neither will he or she direct anyone to you, some can even write a bad review of your product and once that is done online, pray to God to succeed with the sales because due to the scam associated with the internet no one will ever near your eBook link talk more of buying if they notice the bad review. Competition exists and they can easily switch to another eBook rather than risk to buy what has fault.

Next after you must have finished writing and compiling your eBook. There are various ways to sale it as to make money online. You can publish it with Amazon free publishing system (www.createspace.com), which gives opportunity of publishing and selling both soft and hard copies on Amazon, who takes over the stress of sales, handling and shipping and all you do is to market your eBook. In addition to selling your eBook, you can create a website or blog and install it as an e-commerce on your website or blog using one of the internet payment processing systems. People will have to pay with their credit card after, which the eBook will be downloaded to their email, while the payment system takes its percentage and give you your own though, that depends on the plan you choose. Some plan gives you opportunity of paying monthly and with that no money will be deducted from their sales. To generate more sales, you can also write about the book and all it covers in brief then clearly state how much the book cost and your account number where the money can be paid. This can be a private or company account. So when payment is made and payment details sent and confirmed, all you do is go online and send the eBook to the customer's emails.

So simple and easy way to operate and make money online since you won't have to think of printing talk more of shipping. The above also applies to selling software and websites online. Think you a good idea that could solve problem and set it in form of software. Example is Microsoft word. You realize that sometimes when one makes mistakes with spelling; it tends to correct the writers English, that's solving a big problem. Think of which you can design and start selling to make money online

Chapter Nine

Selling and hosting websites
and domain names

Designing, selling and hosting website is another recommended means of making lots of money online. Starting with designing and selling of websites, internet business is booming and so is website, which serves as the web store. Anyone that operates internet business or makes money online should have a website and that has raised the level of website requirement on the internet making it a good money making business on the internet. You can sell and host turnkey websites or customized websites. Turn key websites are websites that are designed and sold to more than one person with everything the same; articles, header, ads and so on. What the seller does when someone purchases the website is to copy the website files and send or host while he retains the original website file for sale to another person while customized website does not allow it. With customized website all the content will be unique and original; articles, header e.t.c, which is why customized website is more costly than turnkey websites. Turn key website is more or less a scrap. Also be careful even when you want to buy customized website because turnkey website can be sold as original website.

Imagine the seller had sold like hundred copies before you bought yours and everything the same, is obvious the website is a scrap especially when articles plays a great role in establishing websites on the internet. The website can be revived by re-writing all the articles so it can be different and unique from other same articles. Changing the header and other duplicate designs as you saw fit make it unique. Good website designers' buys such then revive it and sell it back at a great price.

In designing a website, there are many tools and websites for free website design. Personally, most easy to operate is www.wordpress.com with wordpress; you don't need to worry about coding because everything is already installed. Every article you publish has social media plugins attached to it so you don't have to bother with designing or coding. Another software tool is adobe Dreamweaver, which is a great tool for easy design of website. It best fits newbie in web designing, who cannot code a full website so uses Dreamweaver as a fast copy and paste tool. In addition to designing and selling websites, you can as well as buy from people and re-sell. It's obvious some people do not know the value of their website as the sell and some might be in need of money or lacks money to maintain the website thereby selling it off cheap. Search for such websites, you can do research on Google. Buy them and work on it and resell it, you can even search for cheaper websites, buy and map it out for sale immediately at another website increasing the price tag.

I will also advice that you attend web designing or development school as to fully tap into the booming business.

If you cannot design a website but has the passion and hopes to learn please, do try because the business of designing and selling website online is booming financially. Money associated with web designing might somehow be on the high side due to its benefits but if you can afford and learn very well then the sky will be your limit with making money. Making sure you have idea and passion for web design before you enroll or else you might be wasting your time and money without understanding anything since coding in web designing is technical.

In addition to making money with web designing, apart from selling the websites, you can design website on lots of niche and promote them and make money from its Google adsense, affiliate marketing and infolink. One website is enough to earn you thousands of dollars on weekly or monthly bases talk more of when you operate and promote more than one, that's double upon double financial freedom. Make sure to finish the first one completely first before jumping to another.

Chapter Ten

How to make money selling and hosting domain names and website

In full understanding of domain name and web hosting and how to make money from it, know that every website is identified on the internet with a domain name and for every designed website to appear on the internet as well as be recognized by search engines, it must be first hosted along with a domain name. Designed websites are just combination of files including photos, text, banners, and header and so on. The files can be viewed online when clicked on after it must have been hosted on the internet with a domain name through web hosting companies.

Further, like what I said about turnkey websites, since its files, the seller can keep replicating it, host and sell to people while he stores the original copy.

Making money with web hosting is a great way of making money online. To set up web hosting business online and make money, you need to first register with re-seller plan as a re-seller with major hosting companies. Like I said earlier never stop using Google to search for any website you need. Go to Google and search for "Best web hosting company with re-seller plan" simply and Google will feed you with lots of websites, go through them and register starting with their level of search rank. Before you register, bear in mind that there is an account fee depending on your plan but it's worth it, that's when you calculate how much you will be making hosting websites with the account based on your own stated fee. For example, if you pay like 300 dollars and able to host atleaste 10 websites at the cost of 5 dollar per month for, which allowed payment is one year upfront. That will be 60 dollars per website and 600 dollars for the 10 hosted websites, which can run into hundreds when you start. That's double your investment and the hosting is renewal every year meaning that once you have good operations, so will you have customers for life for the will keep renewing. That's what makes it more fruitful and beneficial because it's not like selling of products for, which can be bought once and forgotten but for web hosting it must be renewed every year.

Furthermore, when you must have registered as well as made the necessary payment, your account will be created. That will give you the opportunity to host more than one website with your account. The plan was to cover people with lots of website, which could be cost-wise hosting and managing them differently added to the charge of hosting one website. People now converts it into making money by posing as web hosting company then using their re-seller account to host more website based on their own price quote. Some can buy at the rate of 1 per dollar and host for others at the rate of 5 dollar per website. The financial benefits of hosting made web designers to venture into the business of hosting too since there designing skill is an advantage why because anyone that designed website from them can as well be willing to allow them host it.

You can now imagine how much money people make online doing what the like.

Make sure to map out your own hosting plans and prices after, which you start promoting your hosting account link and the more you attract more visitors the more money you will be making every years renewing their accounts.

HOW TO MAKE MONEY ONLINE FREELANCING

A freelancer is an independent individual that engages in any form of making money online and are hardly full time staff. Freelance can be better understood as a contractor, who can work on its own to make money as well can be contracted within time gap to carry out an assignment, it could be writing of article, designing of website, creating back links, hosting website and so on.

Freelancing does not even need a landing page to operate just that it's advisable to have one for reference purpose especially to your future clients. There are

lots of websites like
www.fiverr.com
www.elance.com. Fiverr is a
platform where anyone can buy
or sell one services or the other
for 5 dollars. For example; if you
are good in writing good article
with search keywords. all you do
is register, go to your dash
board and start publishing what
you can do like "I can write an
original article with good search
keywords for 5 dollar" newbie
can use "I can write articles for
5 dollars", that's good too but
versatile but using original and
search keywords sent home a
message that you really know
about search engine

optimization in writing articles and next is you seeing a message that you are contracted to write, which will be first paid to fiverr.com and gets to you when the transaction is successful from both end. So applies to elance.com too just that its fee is beyond that of fiverr, with elance an article project can stand at about 100 to 150 dollars depending. And when you apply and get accepted, what you do is go through the stated works to be done and choose the one you can work on, it could writing of article, it could web designing, it could product and services promotion and so on. In addition to making money as a freelancer, you can write articles and post on Google adsense blogs that when people clicks on your article, you get paid. It happens that you help the write not only writing of good articles but attracting of visitors through the articles and for that the website owner will share percentage of the generated income with you. Like I said earlier, there is no need for blog or website since all you do is within the website, which contains your account and store. Freelancing is jack of all trade business and one of the good ways of making money on the internet.

Chapter eleven

How To Make Money Online Blogging

Blogging is all about writing; it could be articles, stories, proposals, product and services review e.t.c on a particular or general topic. You can write for people and be paid or maintain a blog/website filling it with original articles then, make money from it through Google ad sense and affiliate marketing. Though, to become a successful blogger, you need to discover you passion for writing. In addition, "Are you passionate about writing"? You have to answer the question truthfully before aspiring to make money as a blogger online. And writing is not just writing English, you need to understand English language ethics like when to use punctuation, question mark, spelling e.t.c. though, all those is prioritized if you will write for other people since everyone

needs the best services.
Blogging can be sometimes hard
due to the level of English
writing requirements but once
you withstand the storm, wow,
you will see that blogging is
sweet and fetches lots of income
on the internet.

Meanwhile, among all the
strategies of making money
online blogging is one of the
viable ways of making extra
income on the internet doing
what you love to do. Below are

the various ways a blogger can make money writing online.

Maintain A Website or blog

To make money online as a blogger, it's advisable to own a website or free blog where you post your write ups for the masses to read. To earn income with it; just register the web page with Google adsense and gets paid when someone clicks on Google adverts displayed on the blog/website. Register with internet affiliate marketing companies and earn commissions when people purchases products or services through your blog.

Join Freelance Websites

Another way of making money as a blogger and freelancer is registering with paid writing companies. All you do is register with freelancer websites where writing jobs will be posted with price tag, go through and see the ones you can handle and bid. Some you will upload your articles and get paid based on the traffic and views it generated, others you can write and sale out rightly at a huge fee. Freelancer pays more once there are jobs than normal daily job and its stress.

Write For Online Magazines/Newspapers e.t.c

As a blogger you can make money online writing for internet magazines and newspapers on part time bases or as you saw fit. There are lots of online magazine, newspapers and writing platforms that require the services of writers for their various online activities. Writing jobs online is booming because every single promotion of any business, blog, websites, goods and services on the internet must be through writing.

Chapter Twelve

Comprehensive List Of ways For promoting your website/Business

Meanwhile, from experience, there are various awesome means of creating awareness as well as promoting website, which is where the success of any website lies. It's advisable to understand the various ways very well, which is fun too. Just like updating social media pages, commenting on known issues e.t.c. So just take not of the brief explanation and do as it states as well as keep carrying out further research so as to stay fully updated. The below listed ways will play a great role in not only promoting your website but will generate more income for you.

Expect 99.9% result in your website exposure and sales when you strictly apply the below stated ways of promoting a website and never stop contacting me when necessary

1. Join Affiliate Marketing Program

Affiliate marketing is not only a way of making money online; it also creates awareness about the website as well as boosts its search engine optimization. Sometimes, I imagine how many websites or blogs that exists without monetizing the website with affiliate marketing. Imagine how much that can be spent on Google adword e.t.c and other SEOs in the name of boosting the website compared to when the website is marketed with the affiliate links. It does not only generate visitors, it establishes income and high promotion. So in addition, to making money online with affiliate marketing, it can as well serve as a great promotion tool for the website/blog at an awesome benefit. Promote your website today as to create lots of backlinks.

2. Publish An Article

Writing a good and original article on your niche and publishing it on your site as well as sending it to subscribers of your newsletter is a great way of generating good traffic. You will be surprise as many of them will link back to you. But first make sure that the article is outstanding and insightive why because I don't think your subscribers subscribed to your newsletters or visits your site just to read crab. Make sure to choose awesome topics to write on or review.

3. Attach Signature Link

Ensure to attach your website signature in all your outgoing mails, articles, comments on forums and social media. Know that it will make it possible for all those activities re-direct back to your website, which will speedily raise the website search engine rank. On your own imagine how many back links that is established in such ways. So make a signature link for your website today. In simple terms; signature is a link perhaps, your direct website link to home page or particular article or topic on the website.

4. Post in Question And Answer Groups

Yahoo! Answers is a good example of where to generate large traffic by answering peoples question and leaving your link behind for further reference. You can also come up with a question and in line of the conversation leave your link behind.

5. Submit Your Site To Social Bookmarking Websites

In addition to promoting the website it's good to submit your great web pages on quality social booking marking websites like dig.com and stumbleupon.com while you post any article, make sure its articles or content that is qualitative enough to attract traffic to the website RSS feed.

6. Become An Active Blogger

Being active blogger is another great way of driving traffic to your website. Try to comment a lot on blogs. Many blooggers loves to see their blog updated with new comment. And when you comment and leave your backlink be sure that many will return back the favor. Make sure to share active topic and you can find next topic that might receive large traffic at dig.com

7. Start A Blog

No matter your kind of business, have a blog for your site where you make lots of writings on articles. that will in return help you engage with your customers as well as build your writing skills and ability to create new content on weekly or monthly bases.

8. Be Vocal About Your Opinion

To promote your website seek for forum or social media discussions on your niche where comments or responses are somehow out of point. And you as an authority on the field seize the opportunity to strongly air your view or impactful advice with a link back to your website and imagine how many people that will click on the link. That's the secret of generating clicks from commenting and not just commenting for commenting and site promotion sake.

9. Answer a Question

Just like being opinionated, also promote your website by answering questions on your particular niche on forums and social media. Example is yahoo Answers. But make such to respond to recent comments so it might be voted high thereby generating more views and link back. Answering questions is sometimes more easier than promoting with articles which need more words and writings

10. Make a Creative 404 Page

Making a Creative 404 Page makes it possible for you not to lose visitors as well as generate new ones when the hit your website error page perhaps, due to system malfunction. I believe you must have once clicked on a website but was shown an error page. It emanates from the hosting company perhaps, when they might be working on the website, so configuring the website will help you not lose traffic but can generate new ones too, who might copy the website from the error page

11. Try Opt-In Forms

Think of trading links with an industry in a familiar company that does not compete with you. Still yet, if you can endure it, try with the decision of trading the establishment of a little opt-in form on one of every of your confirmation pages. By that means whenever anybody buys from that other store, the buyer will have the alternative of subscribing for your newsletter, or something else more traffic oriented. The consequences being, that you will need to subdue your visitors into dealing with the feared opt-in form on your confirmation page. You may consider reducing the negative impact by entering the opt-in form on the very last page, so that everything is intact and nothing crashes in case the user closes the window mistakenly.

12. Maintain A Product Review Column

Endeavour to create a review column as well as a side bar in your website or blog where you review products and services or stores on weekly basis. It does not only generate traffics through the thread, it converts traffics to customers who might make purchases. Know that it's good to review products you are well familiar with if not used the product or services already. The generated thread is a great link.

13. Keep Post New Articles

Write original articles in your respective domain name or field. It could be your website article content, have the articles submitted to lots of articles directories. But be double sure that the selected articles to be promoted must be on a well searched and valued topic; otherwise your information might be sent on other sites under your name with no way of correcting any errors in the article. Please, make your content is original and keyword filled or you might be wasting your time all the while for the duplicate can be easily detected and devalued

14. Tap From Press Release

In regards to website promotion, it's advisable to write rich note worthy news press release for your website or content it promotes and submit them to a high search engine ranking press release website. If the article is original and insightive enough it might be selected and published to the news group audience and you can imagine how many traffic and sells that might come from that.

15. Pay Per Click Option

Pay per click is another awesome way of generating traffic and sales but at a paid fee. Pay per click is not free like others but the fact is with the tool you stand to generate great qualitative traffic. This is why you need to understand keywords and how it works when applying for Pay per Click because you need to direct your traffic to direct keywords of your website. For example you can pay for PPC on the instruction that who dare clicks are those that are highly interested in your advertized niche like business for example. What Google will do is to advertize the link in a business platform and communities making sure the right people are generating. When you pay for PPC you are helping some else make money online with Google adsense. PPC is advisable when you cannot promote your website yourself as well as when you need greater visitors. You can use Google adwords, ad center, and e.t.c for generating traffic through PPC.

16. Start an RSS Feed

Really Simple Syndication (RSS) is an awesome means of getting subscribers to view new articles on a current basis. As you set up an RSS feed, visitors can easily subscribe for your RSS feed so as to stay up to date with your content, which will even rise new sign up rank as well as emails subscriptions but make sure your feed satisfies the visitors primary needs and do install your RSS feed where people can easily see them.

17. Start a Mailing List

Meanwhile, you can start with your normal email inbox contacts, select those that might be interested and starts telling them about your web pages or articles on weekly or monthly basis. Do also bear in mind that email newsletter have its laws, which mostly frowns at unsolicited mails, which are sometimes completely out of line as well as a crab thereby messing up peoples mail inbox with good ones. Even if it's possible, allow confirmation of emails from subscribers before initiating any mail conversation for it can land you into deep trouble with internet regulators.

18. Install a Bookmark-This-Page Link

To generate great traffic, it's advisable to remind your visitors about bookmarking your web page. That will help them locate the web page easily should the computer switches off mistakenly. And should the act like me then lots of your web pages will be bookmarked but endeavor to make sure that the page and title to be book marked is awesome and outstanding. That will encourage them the more.

19. Design a Good Favicon

An awesome favicon portrait achieves lots of positive impact for your website; it does not only increase your product and services awareness creation, it makes your site to be exceptional among the rest as well as affords your site that exposure that comes along with a well designed favicon file. Though, you should not make the mistake of designing it in animated gif style. Some thought is awesome but know that some had deleted a bookmarked site because of the favicon symbol nature. Just don't even think about it.

20. Submit Your Site to Internet Directories

Internet Directories are some of the great ways of generating quality and good link backs. It will only require your time dedication as to be able to manually register with all the directories. As a starter I will advise you start with free ones and upgrade to paid plan when you must had understood how it works.

21. Submit Your Blog to Blog Directories

Like generating traffic from submitting to internet directories, it's great to submit to blog directories too. The good about blog is that apart from submitting to website directories it can also be submitted to blog directories, which implies double back links but like I said earlier on the previous number; make sure to have the time because it sometimes gets boring. Know that the impacts like traffics and sales it worth it.

22. Advertise on Craigslist

If you haven't heard of craigslist is another awesome search engine ranking website for submission of site for free. But know that you can have the opportunity of tapping from the traffic only if you can write quality post, which are original and insightive enough to go viral online. To succeed with craigslist, create an attractive as well as catchy title and key worded body and conclusion with links back to your site. But no matter what, don't waste your time by spamming with worthless ads or duplicated posts because you might be wasting your time.

23. Use a Tell-a-Friend Script

Just like "share" or "like" on the social media. When you install the "Tell-a-friend" link on your site, you stand the chance of have a visitor promoting your link to potential friends, who will in turn suggest to other friends as it keeps going round. That's an awesome way of attracting great traffic to your site to the general public

24. Submit Your RSS to Feed Directories

A professional might think I forgot this one. Just like how you submitted to other directories try to also submit your RSS to feed directories as to keep attracting huge traffic for your website. Directories are one of the ways of generating visitors.

25. Submit to Whatever Directory You See, For Whatever Reason

Nevertheless, in order to keep increasing your website traffic, it will be advisable to keep submitting your site to directories of your niche you comes across. That will increase your website traffic the more as well as generates sales. So look for quality directories and keep submitting your site

26. Teach a Class

No, really. Though, I depend on your passion but with a good degree you can. Through the teaching you can have your name established within your class and community and so is your website link. It might not pay well but you need the traffic itself. Depending on your niche, you can post an assignment on the site and direct student there for answer in addition t that, since you will be dealing with adult student, it's possible that many will opt in as to generate extra income thereby giving the opportunity of attracting traffic and income at the same time directly from them and their down line. .

27. Create a Cartoon Mascot

Cartoon mascots could be good when they're applied according to legal settings. Cartoons generate various types of people and not just kids alone. Studies certify that eyes are more attracted to cartoon than it's attracted to simple logos. Create a good cartoon as an ad for promoting your link, and then have it spread out to the public.

28. Install Game Contest

It's a fact that games generate great traffic. You can source for a minimal budget contest game of about two people for your website. The game can keep bringing them back to your website even with other friends thereby attracting more traffic for you. Also don't forget to submit the game to games directory sites for more traffic.

29. Sell on eBay

Trading on eBay does expand your ways of making selling your items it attracts lots of link back to your website. Besides, your profile is already a permanent page on eBay, which must contain you site links. And the more you drive sales through eBay, the more link backs you attract and be sure that eBay is one of the great sites that are spidered by Google couple of times each day, which assures you that every back link counts in search engine page ranking. Talk more of the new audience to be drive through eBay

30. Keyword Articles

To drastically increase your website or blog exposure and search engine rank on the internet, make sure to keep publishing original articles on it. You need to write or employ someone else to write original articles for you perhaps, reviewing your website and the product and services it promotes using good search keywords. For better understanding of the activeness of keywords in search engines; for example if words that are well search online by people depending on your niche is "How to lose weight" which records 80 percent clicks while "Ways to lose weight" records 50 percent. Definitely, it's obvious that if your writer does not understands that and keeps using ways to lose weight so will it be having 50 percent view compared to when joined with "How to lose weight. That's just an example for it can come in many forms; it could used in form of single word. For example; "A" have more click percentage compared to "An" which is why you see many writers use "A" rather "AN" before a vowel sound (e.g. "An" aeroplane is now changed to "A" aeroplane). Though, it's an

English error but the writer needs the clicks and search engine rank upgrade. Those are the technicalities of promoting website or blog I want you to understand because those are the success of all the successful website you saw online making thousands of dollars. You can better imagine how much clicks or internet traffic and money your website or blog could be generating on daily, weekly or monthly basis if it's published with articles that reflects the above idea. That will not only boost your sales income, it will also rank your website position high on search engines like

Google, bing e.t.c. And when it happens, you won't have to source for customers or clients anymore as they will keep coming through the established tactics and so is the payment too.

31. Join Online Forums/Communities

Participating actively on internet forums and discussion communities is one of the ways of directing customers and traffic to your online business blog. Though, you MUST make sure to join public communities or forums that deal on what you promote so you can be interacting with likeminded individuals. Don't promote weight loss products or services and go join political forum to discuss weight loss issues. That might not work or generate the needed customer because you will like who visits your blog or website today to come back again, which is why you need to know what they want and post exactly that they wish to read or see.

This is how you can generate customers and traffic by joining forums pertaining to your niche. Public forums are were people interacts as well as seek information so let's say you promote as well as maintain a blog on weight loss and having registered with a particular forum it must happen that within all the posted threads, some might have issues or questions about how to lose weight or burn fat. Being that the topic is what you are well conversant with as well as covers what your web page promotes, what you do is to explain in brief about the asked question on the forum, then, leave behind a re-direct link to an article on your website where the question is fully explained. Once you had the right answers, the person asking the question and people that might hope to have such question answered must definitely keep clicking on the link you left behind so as to read and understand more. Imagine how much customer and money you can be making on daily, weekly and monthly basis consistently if you are able to share as well as post your links to lots of public forums.

In addition to answering people's questions, you can write a review with links about the product and services your website or blog promotes and publish it on forum too so people can easily click as the read.

Further, so how do you get the websites of forums where to share your links and posts? What to do is go to google.com search engine and search for forum websites based on your domain. For example if your website is about weight loss search for weight loss forums, which you can easily generate by typing "Best weight loss forums" on Google and click search. Google will display lots of forums on weight loss, you can checkmate the ones with good traffic and write them down and register later or you can click and register right away but endeavor to visit the forum once in a while as to comments and spread your links until it starts attracting visitors or traffic on its own. This is why you must understand your selected niche very well so you can freely write on it always.

32. Write your website link anywhere possible

Physically, you can create mini sign board, banners and leaflets with you domain name clearly written on it, advertizing the product and services your web page promotes. These can be pasted on the walls of people crowded places. It can be shared to people as well as left behind perhaps, in a bus as you come out e.t.c. make sure the internet link is clearly displayed on it. Even if you cannot afford money for the advert expenses, Chalk or charcoal should be enough to help you write the link on walls of crowded place like markets, parks, roads. It can be better down at night or earliest morning to avoid public notice. Know that with the level at, which people have access to internet so will the easily copy the link and checked it out for, which there are possibility the clicks can turn to sales and money.

33. Social Media

I believe you have account with the social media like face book, LinkedIn, twitter, which now plays a great role in generating huge traffics to websites/blog. Just the way you update your status on social media, channel your writings towards your website article link, you can also share all your articles on your social media for which only the topics will be displayed and who wants to read more must click on it to be directed to your website. It's advisable you create a new page for the website or blog using its domain name then add as much people as you can as well as encourage them to share your post so it can be seen by their own networks, who can connect with your activity. Spreading your link must be your priority since there lays the future benefits and success of any internet website and business. Write, write and write

34. Create App for your site

Meanwhile, in the quest of attracting large traffic, it's important to note the great role an app for your site can play in it. With the rise in smart and android phones, which works perfectly with applications, many now prefer browsing sites through their android applications. Apps are not only clear and concise when browsing with them it portrays a high level of interactivity for the user at a speed rate. It's also accessible and easy to use and people don't have to save or bookmark your site, all the do is click on the site app logo and it connects. And since it's boldly stored on the phone home page the user can easily find and click on it while accessing the phone.

35. Use Business Cards Aggressively

It's obvious that many neglects this methods perhaps, since it's an online business stuff forgetting that it is the traditional human beings that made the internet activities possible. So if you don't have a business card now and you really need traffic then, you have to consider one. Just have your website name well stated on the designed business card and have it shared to family, friends, relatives and the general public. You can even initiate a discussion on your niche within few people and end up with your card in their hands. Know that some takes it serious as well as browses the site. Some might browse for browsing sake but gets to like what they see. That way you can attract large visitors as well as traffic thereby generating sales and SEO

36. Cross-Promote Your Pages

You can attract great visitors cross-promoting your web pages. That is linking up other content of your website as you write an article explaining an issue. For example, let's say you have an article with the topic; "How to burn calories" and you are writing a new article on "How to lose weight" along the line as you write the article, you can get to a point where you can be like. "For more information on how to lose weight by burring calories click here. That's cross-promoting pages and people will definitely take a look since calories are great part of fat forming in the body. So use the example on your site and imagine how only one person can keep rotating within your site with lots of different clicks

37. Purchase Misspelled Domains

Purchasing of misspelled domains can be applied when you have major competitors in your selected domain. The duty of the misspelled domain names on your competitors is to re-direct their traffic to your site.

What you do is to first find out your competitor misspelled domain name. For example, the competitor website domain name is www.hubwell.com and people do search www.hubwell.net thinking it .net. You can buy the second domain name and have it re-directed to your website along with its traffic. That will help you tap from your own traffic and that of your competitors, which gives you a better leverage on search engines and that of your competitors

38. Advertise on Bulletin Board Sites

Just like we have traditional notice boards look for targeted markets on bulletin board site where people of your niche gathers and mount your site board; some can be free and some might be paid plan. Is obvious that since it's what goes along with what the people needs; definitely there will be clicks because people never stops seeking information. Just find awesome bulletin board sites on your field and advertize your site and make sure to advertize something catchy like codes for discounts or special offers to member's benefits.

39. Donate time or resources

Generating traffic through charities is another awesome ways of driving customers to your business. Know that the charity organization cherishes by sitting your link on their mailer and website and it's well appreciated.

40. Build small web tools

Just like offering contest game on your site, offering web

applications for your customers on your site will also keep bringing the customers back and can also make it possible for your website to be indexed of list of web apps.

41. Synergy with other sites

Partnership in awareness creation of an online business or website link with other sites to offer your services in tandem is very important. Why because it does not only give you access to their customer base, it showcases your services and content to another lots of new customers.

42. Viral marketing

Go Viral in promoting your website. That's come up with innovative ways of promoting your website like participating in contests, which can generate traffic, trying to maintain a cordial interaction and relationship with your customers by advancing your customer care method. With viral marketing, you can have your website highly well exposed on the internet.

43. Think Locally

Meanwhile, since internet business affords you the opportunity of trading with people around the world, it will be an added advantage and credit if you go local by setting up a local business name for your site with the help of the local chambers of commerce. It will to a large extend drive you traffic as well as establish networking with your friends and peers in your local area.

44. Update Regularly

What is constant is change. That means that for anything to survive or succeed there is need for regular update as to adapt to change, which is constant. If you reach people through mail, make sure to have them update with your newsletter least once in a month but weekly is better. And for your website content and articles try to update them constantly since it's obvious that what happened in 2013 cannot still be the same in 2015. That's the secret of retaining your old customers and traffic while driving new ones as well as makes your articles outstanding among your competitors but first bear in mind that you will write and write again and again.

45. Contract an SEO Specialist

You can drive great traffic to your business by hiring a professional search engine optimizer of websites, who can promote your website by applying lots of SEO tools like back links repair and monitor, website security and other lots of internet tools for professionally promoting a website. Paying an SEO expert works a lot just that it will only cost you money for the services but be assured that when you are sleeping they are fixing your website and business to keep making money online.

46. Publish to Article-seeking Site

You can generate massive traffic by posting on article-seeking site. Like ezinearticles; they have traffic but don't have the required articles needed in updating their site. So when you publish on their site you have the opportunity of sharing your website content with other sites and receives great back link in return

47. Join a trade group

Make sure to cooperate as well as relate with people running the same website as yours. Try to advertize with one another and also network together in offering your customers awesome customer care services. That will afford you a great opportunity of promoting your website.

48. Offer special deals to your customers

Offering special deals and discount for your customers is a great way of generating traffic because nobody that does not like good thing especially when it has to do with money. Like myself; I had to offer a hosting fee of 8 dollars per month to 1.99 dollars per month for 1 year. That will not only retain old customers but will keep generating new ones thereby drastically promoting the website on the internet.

49. Optimize your site for search engines

Optimizing your website search engine is a great way of attracting good traffic. It obvious that lots of internet users today uses search engines like Google and yahoo to seek information from websites, which makes it the most adored means of driving visitors. You can optimize your website search engine rank using keywords and Meta tags. That will speedily promote your website.

50. Hire an SEO specialist

When you must had applied all your own SEOs ideas, it will be great to contract an SEO professional who is more advanced than you to still work on the website SEO. That will be another good way of promoting your website. Know that SEO never stops for any website or competitors will overtake you.

51. Break a Record

Go for gold; make name by accomplishing something that seems impactful with your website. That will gets you more traffic and besides, lots of news agencies can hardly publish an article of an obscure website and record.

52. Ask your customers

Seeking your customers opinion on how to serve them better gives them a great sense of belonging as well as more encouraged to come back even with someone else. On your part, the customer's feedback and ideas must give you some clue of how to operate an awesome business site

Chapter Thirteen

Search Engine Optimization Websites

Analyzed are sections of website search engine optimization with website links where you can generate good traffic for your site.

Online Directories

Online directories are one of the great ways of attracting great visitors from search engines like Google and yahoo. It's obvious that almost the whole of internet users visits websites or accesses websites information through search engine. That means that publishing your link on search engines can speedily increase your website ranking and visibility on the internet.

Use the links below to register your website with the most

advanced and most patronized search engines in the world.

1. www.google.com/local/add
2. www.local.yahoo.com
3. www.bing.com/businessportal
4. www.dmoz.org
5. www.merchantcircle.com/corporate

Social Media Bookmarking

Submitting website for bookmarking on booking

marketing site is another great way of generating as well as driving huge traffic to your website. The websites will help people to easily bookmark or pinpoint your article for easy retrieval next time. You can succeed with book marking sites when you post articles with good originality as well as full of readers needed information. By that way your visitors can easily bookmark your post, which will serve as gate way into your website. People love to bookmark good articles so the wont lose it and its information in future. In addition to that, the level of information contained in the article will even encourage the visitor to keep visiting your site knowing fully well what to get from it. That will be a great way of driving good traffic or visitors to your website thereby increasing your sales and commission.

Below are the listed sites where you can submit your favorite articles, websites, links and stories for book marking, which is a great way of creating awareness about your original work and afford good back link in return.

1. www.delicious.com
2. www.stumbleupon.com
3. www.Digg.com
4. www.reddit.com
5. www.Pinterest.com

Article Marketing

To drastically increase your website or blog exposure and search engine rank on the internet, make sure to keep publishing original articles on it. You need to write or employ someone else to write original articles for you perhaps, reviewing your website and the product and services it promotes using good search keywords. For better understanding of the activeness of keywords in search engines; for example if words that are well search online by people depending on your niche is "How to lose weight" which records 80 percent clicks while "Ways to lose weight" records 50 percent. Definitely, it's obvious that if your writer does not understands that and keeps using ways to lose weight so will it be having 50 percent view compared to when joined with "How to lose weight. That's just an example for it can come in many forms; it could used in form of single word. For example; "A" have more click percentage compared to "An" which is why you see many writers use "A" rather "AN" before a vowel sound (e.g. "An" aero plane is now changed to "A" aero plane). Though, it's an English error but the writer needs the clicks and search engine rank upgrade. Those are the technicalities of promoting website or blog I want you to understand because those are the success of all the successful website you saw online making thousands of dollars. You can better imagine how much clicks or internet traffic and money your website or blog could be generating on daily, weekly or monthly basis if it's published with articles that reflects the above idea. That will not only boost your sales income, it will also rank your website position high on search engines like Google, Bing e.t.c. And when it happens, you won't have to source for customers or clients anymore as they will keep coming through the established tactics and so is the payment too.

Use the below sites to promote your articles so as to drive good traffic from quality article marketing sites

.

1. www.ezinearticles.com
2. www.hubpages.com
3. www.goarticles.com
4. Article Dashboard
5. www.businessknowhow.com

Press Releases

Press releases are a great way of introducing your website, product or services to the general public. In regards to website promotion, it's advisable to write rich note worthy news press release for your website or content it promotes and submit them to a high search engine ranking press release website. If the article is original and insightive enough it might be selected and published to the news group audience that's after it's already published on their website by you and you can imagine how many traffic and sells that might come from that.

Use the below website to publish your favorite articles to world rate press release agencies.

1. www.prlog.org
2. www.free-press-release.com
3. www.24-7pressrelease.com
4. www.1888pressrelease.com
5. www.pr-inside.com
(European-based distribution)

In conclusion, do know that apart from the one listed here; there other one you can research up on your own and register. Is all about promoting your website and you needed to push it to the limit so as to succeed? In addition to that, be mindful of your audience

In conclusion

Personally, I believe you must have had some clue about promoting a website as to generate great traffic, sales and money. In addition to that, like I said earlier; never hesitate to contact me for any assistance.

SUCCESS! SUCCESS!! SUCCESS!!!

I wish you success and below are my contacts. Never hesitate to contact me if you need any explanation whatsoever. I design websites, free blog, writes articles just call me a freelancer for all I write here is all am expert on. I know you can do it yourself after reading but if you still need any of the paid services due contact me.

Christopher Obiaku

Phone numbers:
+2348036953673,
+2348095854528
E-mail:
chrisbusinessacademy@yahoo.c
om

www.ingramcontent.com/pod-product-compliance
Lightning Source LLC
Chambersburg PA
CBHW051454170526
45166CB00001B/247